# GOING TO HEAVEN VIA THE PET SHOP

### LYNN McATAMNEY
**Illustrated by Tilly Scribbles**

"How will Rollie get to heaven?" asked the four-year-old boy.

"Well," I said.

"We will take him to the vet,
and cuddle him until it is time to leave.

The vet is very kind and knows how much we love Rollie. She will give him special medicine to put his body to rest."

"So will Rollie go to the pet shop and then to heaven?" the boy asked.

"Mmm . . ." I said. "The pet shop is different to the vet, but I know what you mean!

The vet is a person who looks after animals. She has helped Rollie stay healthy for a long time. But now his body is starting to hurt too much.

When we take him to the vet to say goodbye, it's another way to show Rollie we love him."

"But how will Rollie know where heaven is?"
asked the boy.

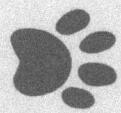 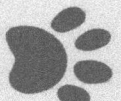
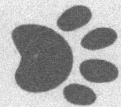

  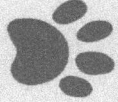

"Rollie always knew how to find his way home.
Maybe it's like that. I'm sure he will find his way there."

"Where is heaven, Grandma?" asked the boy.

"It's where we go when we finish using our body," I explained.

"Soon, Rollie will be free from his tired old body.

We can say thank you for our time with Rollie, and ask God to look after him for us."

A few days later, the boy thought about the times he had played with Rollie, and how his tail would go around and around in circles whenever he got excited.

"I wish I could see Rollie," the boy said.

"Me too," I replied, "but we can remember the happy times we had with him."

The boy's eyes lit up.

"Remember when he chased the ball into the lake and almost brought it back to me, but then he stopped and I had to go and get it because he was getting ready to fetch it again?"

"I remember that!" I said. "Let's think about more of those good times, because they keep Rollie connected to us in our hearts."

After a moment, the boy looked up. "Grandma, why did God let Rollie die?"

"God didn't make him die," I replied.
"It was just that Rollie's body didn't work anymore.
It was time for him to go. Rollie's body was wearing out,
and the tablets couldn't stop that."

"Can Rollie come back?" the boy asked.

"No, he will never come back to us," I answered, "and even though we miss him, it wouldn't be kind to bring him back. But Rollie can always remind us how precious people are.

Sometimes we feel cranky or lonely and we forget to be kind . . .

By remembering Rollie, we can choose to give a smile instead of a growl."

"Have you seen the message on my bathroom mirror? I wrote it there so I can see it every day. It says:

DEAR LORD, PLEASE HELP ME BE THE KIND OF PERSON MY DOG THINKS I AM.

The boy thought about that. He remembered that Rollie had always been excited to see him.

"I want to be like Rollie," said the boy. "I want everyone to know how special they are."

"You already do that!" I said with a smile.
"You make me feel very special indeed!"

"Now, would you like to say goodbye to Rollie with me?

We could walk down to the lake
where he loved to swim . . ."

"That is a great idea!" said the boy.

"Can we pick some yellow flowers from the garden for him too?"

"Of course!" I said as I gave him a hug.

"When can we go?"
"Let's ask Mum," I replied.

That afternoon the boy and his
grandma stood by the water's edge.
Suddenly, the boy fell silent.

"I miss Rollie," he said with tears in his eyes.

"I do too," I said.

"We will both have to get used to not seeing him all the time. But just for now, it's okay to feel sad."

Together they bent down and placed a flower on the water.

"Goodbye, Rollie," I said.

"Goodbye, Rollie," said the boy.

The End

Rollie was a gentle boy, until he saw walking shoes or a ball. Then his joy for life would burst forth with an insistence to go walking. 'Life is great, c'mon let's go!' he would say.

In his fourteen years of life, Rollie 'belonged' to two families . . . and our neighbours. Thank you, Rollie, for your trust and love.

Torn Curtain Publishing
Wellington, New Zealand
www.torncurtainpublishing.com

© Copyright 2021 Lynn McAtamney

ISBN Softcover 978-0-6451757-5-2

All rights reserved. No portion of this book may be reproduced, stored in a retrieval system or transmitted in any form or by any means—electronic, mechanical, photocopy, recording or otherwise—without prior written permission of the author.

Typeset in Mr Eaves and Azo Sans

Illustrations by Tilly Scribbles. Used with permission.

Cataloguing in Publishing Data
   Title: Going to Heaven via the Pet Shop
   Author: Lynn McAtamney

A copy of this book is held at the National Library of Australia.

www.ingramcontent.com/pod-product-compliance
Lightning Source LLC
Chambersburg PA
CBHW062044290426
44109CB00026B/2731